Forward by Neville Staple, Th
he Fun Boy 3 and The Nevill

I love travelling around Coventr
think about the places I have
have grown and been creative. Some of these places have put Coventry on the music map. From my own history in music, including 2Tone music which was born right here, through to  the history of bands like the Enemy and even the Beatles local historic moments. This book is fascinating, full of interesting things that would be a perfect tour guide of knowledgeable facts. Check it out and read it while you explore our great City. It would be *'rude'* not to..! **Neville Staple**

About the Author - Pete Chambers BEM

Pete has spent a life in local music, and was honoured in 2015 with a British Empire Medal for services to Coventry Music. In 2017, he was awarded a Point Of Light Award by the Prime Minister and also given an Honorary Doctorate by Coventry University. He currently writes a music column for The Coventry Observer, and is Director Curator at The Coventry Music Museum. He's a regular contributor on radio and TV, has written eight books on local music history. It was Pete who initiated the Coventry Stars, and the 2-Tone Trail and is passionate about new bands and artists coming through on the scene.

Welcome to Coventry
Or Hiya if you already live here

So you have been sent to Coventry, lucky you, so how did you arrive?

By Road

Coventry's ring road is a bit of a local talking point, most motorists are not keen, and many say that it cuts the city off to the outlying areas. That aside it has been immortalised in at least three songs. King first name-checked the road in their song "Fish", Paul King sings, "I've been looking for the heart of town, but the ring road leads me round and round". Punk band TDA once played a gig under it.

In 2014 the Ring Road celebrated its 40th anniversary, we got two tracks dedicated to it. Coventry musician David Goody produced a very tongue in cheek ditty about the road entitled "Rules of the Coventry Ring Road". Later that year Siobhan Harrison of BBC Coventry & Warwickshire, came up with the idea of a song. So a supergroup was assembled that included Special Horace Panter and ex Special Neville Staple and Spooky Wagons as a backing band, with then BBC presenter Shane O'Connor on vocals. The song as chosen in a poll by listeners was a rework of The Average White Band's "Lets Go Round Again".

Also close to the Ring Road is the sports centre in Fairfax St, or The Elephant (from our civic arms). Some say it looks nothing like an elephant, but viewed from the Ring Road it kinda' does. It's either going to be demolished or become a huge area for our amazing artists, I hope for the latter. Music-wise it was featured in the Enemy video for the song "It's Not Ok" (see The Enemy's Coventry). Other music related sites seen from the ring road include The Kasbah, Sky Dome, Coventry University and behind the old toy museum a lane where the Colourfield once posed for a publicity shot .

Extreme right, Terry Hall's Colourfield pose at the rear of the old toy museum near Much Park St. Right, part of the ring road in its new sort of 2-Tone cladding.

Welcome to Coventry By Train

So stepping off the train at Coventry Station you would have followed in the footsteps of millions, so here are some of the stand-out music connections of the station.

On December 17th 1977, the Sex Pistols arrived at Coventry Station in their tour coach (no, I'm not sure why there either), well after a take away meal and a few cans of Breaker, they went off to play at Mr George. The result can be heard on many a bootleg of the gig.

Even stranger was a visit by the godfather of soul, James Brown ya' all in July 16th 2003. He was left stranded at the station after his train had broken down, as he attempted to get to Liverpool for a gig. He was happy to sign autographs for the commuters then ninety minutes later he was "back on the good foot" and in a limo Merseyside bound.

The Specials often did their photo-shoots around the station, as it was near Horizon Studio, Anarchy Bridge often figured as a back drop. See photo below, the bridge is still there, "I have seen the fnords".

Above The Specials on Anarchy Bridge, below left our Sponsor Kev Monks on platform 1, recreating the original Specials pic . Below its Sid and Johnny outside Coventry Railway Station.

Welcome to Coventry By Boat

A less likely way of visiting Coventry, more of a contrivance to include the Canal Basin. The Canal Basin area is well discussed in the 2-Tone Trail (see the 2-Tone Trail). Famous for the locations of The Specials album covers, and the amazing live venue 'The Tin'. What is less known that in 1993 The Specials and Reggae god Desmond Dekker came here to shoot the cover of their Trojan album "King of Kings".

Right, mega rare colour picture of the Specials during the Canal basin cover shoot.

Stand in the footsteps of the Reggae King of Kings Desmond Dekker

Located at the Canal Basin where the cover shots for the "King Of Kings" LP (with The Specials) were shot by legendary photographer Jason Tilley.

Above left is the pic on the CD shot at the rear of the Canal Basin on the bridge at Drapers Field. Picture on the above right is Julie Chambers showing the location now. Pics by Jason Tilley

Welcome to the 2-Tone Trail
Non-plaque 2-Tone sites (marked as letters on map) Part 1

A-Odeon Cinema-(Jordan Well) Dance Craze played here on 3rd March 1981. A well used promotion photo of The Specials was taken on the roof of this building (now fittingly The Ellen Terry Building, a faculty for the performing arts and communications).

B-Oak Inn- (Gosford Street) A central contact point in the formative years for Jerry, Brad and Neol, Neol remembers that the floor was black and white check. It was after a night in here that Jerry came up with the name The Specials.

C-Far Gosford St- see Far Gosford Street map and page

D-Lucas Building-(Read Street) This is now a storage warehouse. The Selecter's Neol Davies worked here. After a very bad day he turned to a female colleague and declared he had 'Too Much Pressure' within a few minutes a great song (and album title) was born.

Above left, The old Lucas building, above right The Oak Inn as it was, bottom Left, The Specials with the Odeon Management outside the cinema entrance.
pic by Chalkie Davies.

The 2-Tone Trail

★	**Walk of Stars**	6	**The Rocket**
1	**The Lanch, Coventry University**	7	**Holyhead Youth Club**
2	**The Hand & Heart**	8	**Mr George**
3	**The Binley Oak**	9	**Tiffany's**
4	**The Canal Basin**	10	**Virgin Records**
5	**51 Albany Road**	11	**The Heath Hotel**

The 2-Tone Trail

THE EMPIRE

The Empire Nightclub and venue, that has hosted the likes of The Enemy, Neville Staple Band and The Primitives.

FARGO

Fargo is an artisan multi-entertainment area with shops and The Box Venue. It also has a Phil Silvers Museum.

The 2-Tone Village was created for fans by fans for all things Ska and reggae. Here you will find: The Coventry Music Museum, The 2-Tone Café, Simmer Down Restaurant, 2-Tone Corner shop, Hall of Fame memorabilia shop, plus the Coventry Music Wall of Fame and The Stars of Ska & Reggae.

40 YEARS OF 2 TONE 1979 - 2019
2 TONE VILLAGE

Welcome to Coventry's famous 2-Tone Trail

Okay, we recommend that before you begin your tour, you visit The 2 Tone Village and the Coventry Music Museum. Here you will get lots of advice and hints for your journey ahead. Please bear in mind, we are presenting the main plaque trail here plus reference to the other 2-Tone sites that didn't receive a plaque. Please note that two of the plaques are long gone (Binley Oak and The Rocket).

The start point of the trail is now located outside of the BBC Coventry & Warwickshire Radio Station, in Priory Place. If you locate the huge Whittle Arches structure, (opposite the Transport Museum) you will find the BBC and The Walk of Stars like a pot of gold at the end of a metal rainbow………………

Coventry Stars and Start Point, (Priory Place) CV6 5SQ

Crossing Priory Place diagonally are The Coventry Stars. Of major interest to 2-Tone fans, will be The Specials and The Selecter stars. Also the bands first real manager Pete Waterman also has a star here. The plaques were unveiled in a big ceremony on 16th May 2008. In attendance for the Specials was Horace and Roddy.

Left, Roddy and Horace, middle Charley, Neol and Gappa of The Selecter accept their stars.
Selecter photo by Covsupport News Service,
Specials photo by Hannah Tobin of BBC Coventry & Warwickshire

1. Coventry University (The Lanch)
Priory Street CV1 5FJ

When you get here your iPod should be playing "Rat Race".

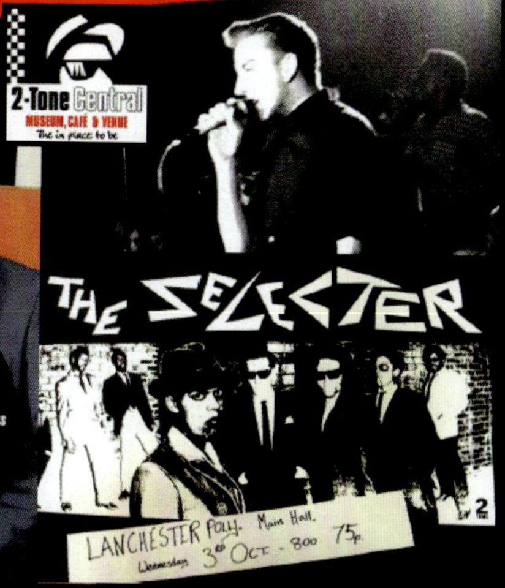

Coventry University, was known as the Lanchester Polytechnic in the days Pauline Black and Jerry Dammers and Horace Panter attended. It was here where Jerry first met Horace, a meeting that proved to be crucial to the creation of The Specials. The song "Rat Race" was conceived here and the promotional video was recorded in the main hall in 1980. The Specials played here in September 1980. The Selecter played this venue in October 1979 and the mark one version of the Coventry Music Museum 2-Tone Central was based here. Jerry Dammers, and Pauline Black have both received Honorary Doctorates from Coventry University.

"Coventry was not just the city where The Specials came from, it was the city that inspired the songs we wrote. Ghost Town, Concrete Jungle, Friday Night/Saturday Morning all had their roots here, and still resonate today as they did 40 years ago"
Horace Panter The Specials

Sponsored by Coventry University
This plaque is located at the entrance to the Student Union Building, Priory Street, opposite the new Cathedral. It was unveiled by **Horace Panter (The Specials)** on 2nd October 2009.

COV TRIVIA-When Jerry originally graduated, he never picked up his degree, in 2005 Jerry was awarded an Honorary Degree, and this time was happy to take it.

2. The Hand & Heart
Far Gosford St CV1 5EA

When you get here your iPod should be playing "Out On The Streets"

The Hand and Heart pub played host to the emerging Coventry punk scene in the late 1970's. Reggae band Hardtop 22 played there, and a few months later key members of the band would form the core of the Selecter. On February 23rd 1978, a band called the Coventry Automatics played the venue, on Friday 1st December 1978 they returned as The Specials.

"I invite everyone who walks this historic trail to reflect on what was at the root of the 2Tone movement: Equality, justice and non-discrimination. These values inspired our original music and continue to drive my life today. Live by them and be free!" **Charley Anderson The Selecter**

Sponsored by Harrabin Construction

This plaque is located on the front of the former Hand and Heart building currently a Pizza Parlour and part of the Fargo Village Development. It was unveiled by the late Steve 'Cardboard' Eaton on 27th November 2009. Steve was the face on the Too Much Pressure album cover and the original 2-Tone DJ.

COV TRIVIA– In the early 70's Gosford St was an area that was full of second-hand thrift shops. It was here most of the 2-Tone bands got suited and booted.

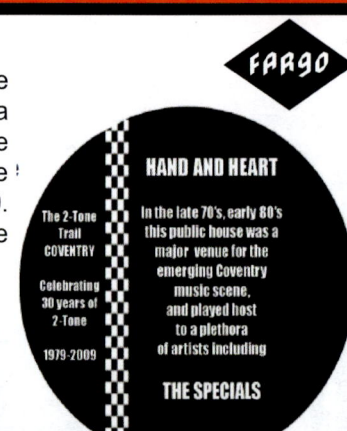

C. FAR GOSFORD STREET (marked as letters on map) Part 2

Far Gosford Street has always had a life of its own, (see Music Mile). Back in the day, it did contain a plethora of second hand (thrift) shops that kept our 2-Tone warriors in tonic jackets and as much collectable vinyl as their Dancettes could cope with. Horace Panter once had a flat in Bramble Street just off Gosford Street (No 70).

Sites in the area were Ramp Studios where the reformed Specials demoed tracks for Today's Specials (upstairs at 139). Hits Misses and Vintage Records was the place to be for Cov record collectors (now a restaurant). Phil Oakey's (Human League) brother Bob once owned a music shop in the street. Tom Clarke of The Enemy had a flat in the area where he wrote "We'll Live and Die" (see The Enemy's Coventry).

FAR GOSFORD STREET

Map not to scale

- The Hand & Heart
- Horace's old flat
- Bramble St
- Ramp studios
- Hits, Misses & Vintage Records
- Vecqueray St
- To City Centre →
- The Empire
- Far Gosford Street
- To Fargo and The 2-Tone Village ←
- All Saints Square
- To Old Lucas Building ↓
- The Beer Engine
- Lower Ford St ↓

'There was talk of buying the old Paris cinema in Gosford Street to convert into a 2-Tone H.Q./studio/club in 1980, it's now The Empire" - Horace Panter. The public house, The Cup (now closed) was the site of Selecter rehearsals, Roddy's Tearjerkers have also played here.

The Hand and Heart pub was an early venue for The Selecter and The Specials also played the venue a few times and as part of their ightening Tour of Coventry in 1978. (see Hand & Heart).

3. The Binley Oak
Paynes Lane CV1 5LL

When you get here your iPod should be playing "The Selecter".

Pic by John Coles

"Rudies don't fail, put Coventry on the map with the 2-Tone Trail".

Pauline Black, The Selecter

Just an ordinary pub in an ordinary street, but the Binley Oak was the prime rehearsal space for the would be 2-Tone artists in the late 1970's. It's where Pauline Black first became a member of the Coventry Ska band The Selecter. It was also here that The Specials first perfected that familiar sound that eventually would become known as 2- Tone. The over-riding memory of the venue was just how cold it was. Horace Panter recalled playing sunny Jamaican ska in fingerless mittens, with frozen fingers. This building is now a school for girls and sadly the plaque is no longer there.

Sponsored by The Binley Oak This plaque is located on the front of this former public house and was unveiled on February 27th 2009 by Pauline Black (Selecter), Neol Davies (Selecter) and Deputy Lord Mayor Jack Harrison.

COV TRIVIA-In the early 70's the back room (see picture above), was known as Motown House, and helped put the pub on the map as a place to go for good sounds.

THE BINLEY OAK

The 2-Tone Trail COVENTRY

Celebrating 30 years of 2-Tone

1979-2009

It was the backroom of this public house that The Specials unique ska sound was originally created and where Pauline Black first became a member of The Selecter

SPONSORED BY
THE
BINLEY
OAK

4. The Canal Basin
Canal Basin CV1 4LY

When you get here your iPod should be playing "Blank Expression".

Black and White photos by Chalkie Davies

Coventry Canal Basin was very run-down the day The Specials arrived for a photo shoot in 1979. It's pretty obvious that neither the band or the photographers Chalkie Davies and Carol Starr, had any idea the images they created that day would become so iconic. Those images graced the front and rear covers of The Specials first album, and the rear of the More Specials LP. Though photographer Chalkie did say, "We always felt that our work for The Specials was the best we had ever done". Jerry wanted the cover to be a pastiche of the Who's "My Generation" LP cover, with the band all looking up at the camera. Today the canal basin is home to many of Coventry's art fraternity and "The Tin" venue and there's actually water in the canal now.

"This is Roddy "Radiation" Byers of The Specials, come and see the home of Two Tone, Coventry an historic city which survived the Blitz and gave birth to the Specials and the Selecter. See the places, feel the vibe"!

Roddy "Radiation" Byers of The Specials

Sponsored by Coventry Market
This was the very first plaque to be unveiled on January 15th 2009. It's located close to the Canal basin mosaic and was unveiled by Roddy Byers (The Specials) and Horace Panter (The Specials).

COV TRIVIA-When you come here check out the iconic photo above on the left, and see if you can recreate it. Send it to us, and we'll give a prize for the best one.

Carole & Chalkie

5. The Birthplace of 2-Tone
51 Albany Road, CV5 6JR

When you get here your iPod should be playing "Gangsters".

Left, Charley Anderson, Pete Chambers and Lynval Golding at 51 Albany Road. Photo By John Cole. Right Jerry back in the day at Albany Rd. Photo by Chalkie Davies & Carol Starr

"The 2-Tone Trail tells the history of the Coventry 2-Tone scene that was created by The Specials and The Selecter. It gives everyone a chance to go around and see where we rehearsed, drank and even slept. I'm extremely proud of it, and I'm sure anyone who travels around the trail will enjoy seeing where some of the songs were written and what was the inspiration to create them. On this trail you will be able to make the connection between the songs". **Lynval Golding The Specials**

51 Albany Road, is the Holy Grail for 2-Tone fans, for it was up in that front-bedroom flat where the 2-Tone phenomenon was born. In 1979/80, it became the HQ of Britain's most creative record label. As well as being Jerry Dammers' home, and a 'hang out' area for the rest of the band. It was featured in the BBC Arena documentary on the rise of 2-Tone, where the band along with Music Journalist Adrian Thrills are gathered in party mood in this one-bedroom record company head-office. It's where the Gangsters V The Selecter sleeves were hand stamped. Don't forget to nip next door for a haircut, like The Specials did.

Sponsored by Pete & Julie Chambers
Although this plaque is a little out of the City Centre in the Earlsdon area, it is an important part of the 2-Tone story. It's worth a visit, to soak up some of that historic atmosphere. This plaque is located on the front of the house under the front bedroom window, the window that was once Jerry Dammer's flat. It was unveiled by Lynval Golding (The Specials) and Charley Anderson (The Selecter) on March 27th 2009.

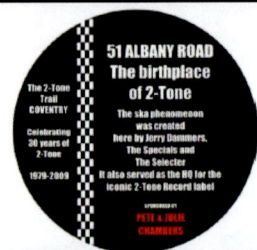

COV TRIVIA- 51 Albany Rd has become a Mecca for fans from all over the world. However this is a private house, be respectful.

6. Horizon Studios/The Rocket
Warwick Road, CV3 6AN

When you get here your iPod should be playing "Stereotype".

Photo by John Coles

Photo right from the archive of Horizon supremo Barry Thomas.

The Rocket public house once bore the plaque that should have been located on Horizon Studios, sadly the studios and indeed the building that housed them has long gone. Horizon studios was very much the tangible face of 2-Tone during its rise to fame. It was here most of The Selecter's body of work was recorded, and of course The Specials first vinyl outing "Gangsters" and their second album "More Specials". Roger Lomas produced Bad Manners here too of course. While The Rocket provided liquid lunches between long recording sessions. The exact location of the studios are where the bollards to the en-trance road to Central Six now lies. Sadly this plaque is no longer there.

"We used to come from Horizon Studios when we had finished recording to here The Rocket, so to me this is where ska really started".
Buster Bloodvessel (Bad Manners)

Sponsored by Shoe Kings (Cov Market)
This plaque is located on the front of this public house and was unveiled by Neville Staple (The Specials) and Mr Buster Bloodvessel (Bad Manners) on May 14th 2009.

COV TRIVIA– In 1980 Pauline Black left the studio whilst recording "The Whisper", and popped down to the Registry Office, got married and returned to her recording duties.

Other non-plaque 2-Tone sites (marked as letters on map) Part 3

E-The Tic Toc- (Primrose Hill Street) A building with a long musical history, became the Orchid Ballroom in the early sixties. It later became The Tic-Toc Club, with more than a little help from Jon Gaunt (now a well know shock jock and TV star). In 1991, it faced closure and a group of 2-Tone people played as part of a benefit evening. The Special Beat also played The Tic Toc (and recorded a live album here), apparently going down as one of the venue's best gigs. It also hosted another conglomerate 2-Tone band in the shape of The International Beat. A reformed Selecter played the venue many times, even hiring it for tour rehearsals and recorded the live album Out On The Streets Again here on 21-12-91. Jerry Dammers had a short DJ residency here in the 90's. It continued to be a house of musical fun as The Colosseum, where on February 9th 2007, The Enemy played A Message To You Rudy and Too Much Too Young, with guest star Neville Staple. The venue has since been reinvented as the Kasbah.

The West Midlands Invader– Suggs in Coventry

Suggs once said "Coventry was in the middle of nowhere". But Madness played Coventry's Tiffany's on 24th April 1980. Suggs was also in attendance when The Specials Played The Lanchester Poly in 1980. The Nutty boys made various journeys to 2-Tone HQ in 1979 and 1980.

Suggs brought his "My Life in Words & Music show to University of Warwick's Butterworth Hall in Feb 2012. In the day he visited The 2-Tone Village, signing the café clock wall. Post show he sang impromptu to a lucky few at The Village Hotel "Big crowd in here tonight" he said, songs included "It Must Be Love" and "Lola". He returned to Warwick University with his "What a King Cnut" show in Feb 2018.

Above Suggs at The Lanchester Bar, below at 2-Tone Village café.

7. Holyhead Youth Club
Holyhead Road CV1 3AU

When you get here your iPod should be playing "(Dawning of A) New Era".

The Holyhead Youth Club and Music Workshop, was where Neville Staple first met the rest of the Specials when they rehearsed in the basement of this club. Coventry Soul singer and 2-Tone catalyst Ray King became the club's manager, Neville Staple and Trevor Evans with their Jah Baddis Sound System, as resident DJ's for the club. The Holyhead became pivotal in the development of the various musicians who would eventually form the 2-Tone bands The Specials and The Selecter. Much of the graffiti from those days is tantalisingly still in evidence on the walls here, making Holyhead Studios a special place for the fan.

"The landscape of our city is changing and some of the historic sites have suffered the fate of the bulldozer and the redeveloper, but thankfully, most remain for future generations. Some of our history and our youth is here before you. I know. I was there..." **Paul Heskett the Swinging Cats & Specials brass**

Sponsored by Harris Signs Group This plaque is located on the front of what is now the Artspace building, it was unveiled on September 11th 2009 by The High Commissioner of St Vincent & The Grenadines Mr. Cenio Lewis KCMG, Coventry Lord Mayor Jack Harrison, Ray King and Neol Davies (The Selecter).

COV TRIVIA– The basement is generally closed, but you may get lucky if you say pretty please to the Artspace staff here.

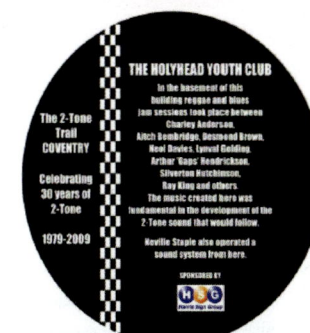

8. Mr George Nightclub

Lower Precinct CV1 1DX

When you get here your iPod should be playing "Man at C&A".

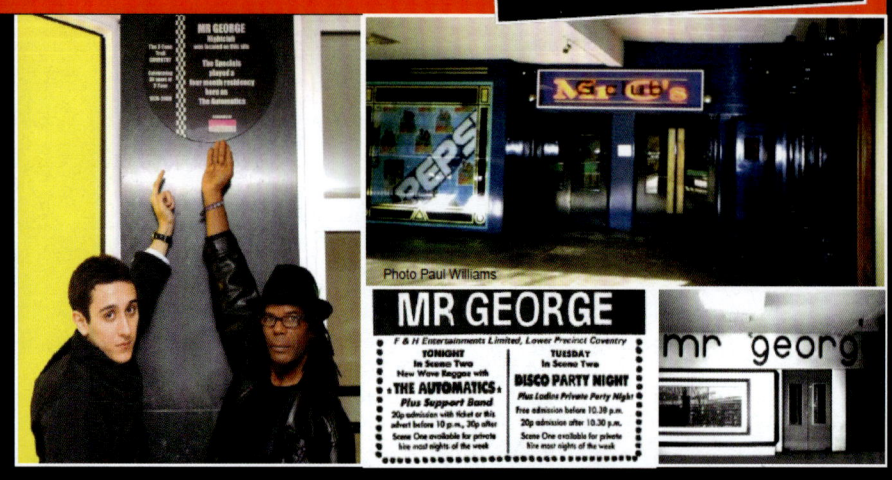

Photo Paul Williams

MR GEORGE

F & H Entertainments Limited, Lower Precinct Coventry

TONIGHT	TUESDAY
In Scene Two New Wave Reggae with **THE AUTOMATICS** *Plus Support Band* 20p admission with ticket or this advert before 10 p.m., 30p after Scene One available for private hire most nights of the week	In Scene Two **DISCO PARTY NIGHT** *Plus Ladies Private Party Night* Free admission before 10.30 p.m. 20p admission after 10.30 p.m. Scene One available for private hire most nights of the week

When The Sex Pistols played at Mr George on 17th December 1977, Jerry Dammers was looking for his band to support them. History tells us that never happened, but that band (The Automatics) did secure a four month Monday night residency here. During that residency, Roddy joined the band, they picked up manager no 2, and supported Ultravox at The Marquee for just £10. Just over a year later , The Automatics had rebranded themselves as The Specials and with the launch of Gangsters ,were enjoying chart success for the first time.

"The 2-Tone Trail is a fine achievement. It celebrates a memorable period in the cultural history of Coventry. This initiative to commemorate the fine work of the 2-Tone artists and their close links with the City is most welcome."
Councillor Tony Skipper

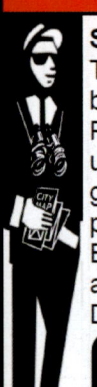

Sponsored by The Lower Precinct

This plaque is located on the upper balcony at the far end of the Lower Precinct under the high rise. It was unveiled on 30th August 2009 by the guys who provide The Specials pre-concert music Felix Hall and Trevor Evans. Trevor was The Specials roadie and Nev Staple's sound system partner, DJ Felix is the son of Terry of course.

COV TRIVIA– Warning, Warning, the shop on the left of the plaque (New Look) was originally C & A, and I don't have a say.

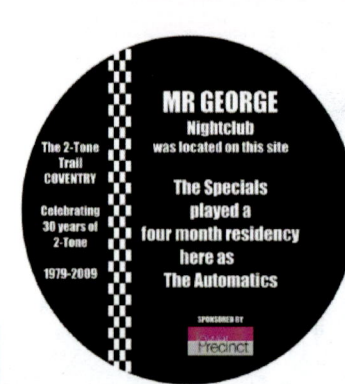

Non-plaque 2-Tone sites (marked as letters on map) Part 4

F-The City Centre Club (now Society, Tower Street). Really just a nightclub (Nite Klub), The Specials and The Selecter played here on 31st July 1979. I remember queuing outside when one of the bouncers had refused Roddy Radiation admission. That was until the whole queue informed the doorman that there would be no concert if he wasn't allowed in! In the hilarious Specials Illustrated Songbook by Nick Davies, Nick illustrates a membership card for the 'City Centre Fite Spot'!

G-The Parson's Nose Chip Shop (Bishop St). A fave' with the club set and local band set in the city, There is a well known picture of The Specials outside the shop indulging in a french fry feeding frenzy, or as Terry Hall puts it in the song Friday Night Saturday Morning. "But 2 O Clock has come again It's time to leave this paradise, hope the chip shop isn't closed cause their pies are really nice". It ceased trading in 2003. The building is now long gone and despite being just a one-off photo location, the Parsons, has featured on at least three Specials TV features. All that remains is the floor tile Jerry stood on owned by the Coventry Music Museum.

9. Tiffany's Nightclub
The Precinct (Smithford Way) CV1 1FY

When you get here your iPod should be playing "Too Much, Too Young".

"Although it reflects the past I think the 2-Tone Trail is still current, and tourists can come and walk it. There are lots of 2-Tone fans from all over the world, and this should bring even more tourists, It's a wonderful thing for Coventry". **Aitch Bembridge, The Selecter**

Pic by Hannah Tobin

Pic John Coles

Tiffany's (or The Locarno or The "Rockhouse"), was a major venue for the city in the 60"s, and 70"s, before it became a public library that is. Chuck Berry recorded his only number one here (My Ding-A-Ling), and all of the major 2 Tone bands played this venue at some time or other (The Specials, Madness, The Selecter, The Beat, The Swinging Cats & The Bodysnatchers). Live B-sides "Skinhead Symphony" The Specials and "Carry Go Bring Home" by The Selecter were both recorded here. The Locarno is also immortalised in the lyrics of The Specials song "Friday Night, Saturday Morning".

Sponsored by CV One
If you look up when you step inside the foyer entrance of what is now Coventry's Central library, you will see this plaque. It was unveiled on July 24th 2009 by Paul Heskett (Swinging Cats and Specials brass), Ranking Roger (The Beat), Aitch Bembridge (The Selecter) and Everett Morton (The Beat).

COV TRIVIA– In 1972 Chuck Berry recorded his chart topper My Ding-A-Ling here, and it remained the last live No1 for nine years, until Too Much Too Young hit the number one spot, the B side also recorded here of course.

10. Virgin Records/Soul Hole
City Arcade CV1 3HX

When you get here your iPod should be playing "Sock It to 'Em JB"

Pic John Coles

In the 70"s Virgin Records provided a base for the music-minded in the city. The late John "Brad" Bradbury, AKA Prince Rimshot, worked here, and developed his love for various forms of music, including reggae, soul and of course ska. The original Coventry Automatics vocalist Tim Strickland, and Swinging Cat Chris Long also earned a wage at the shop. Upstairs the Soul Hole was the domain of Pete Waterman, Locarno DJ and the very first Specials Manager. If you couldn't get it anywhere else, Pete would get it for you here. That's long before he became a global phenomenon of course. The shop is now a Café, but the whole area is destined to be demolished in the near future.

> "As a Coventrian born and bred I am proud of the message of unity the 2-Tone Trail brings to those who walk it. May the Trail go on forever".
> **Brad The Specials**

Sponsored by Kev Monks
The 11th and final plaque to be unveiled as part of the 'Big Launch' of the whole project. What better way than to have Coventry Legends (Specials first Manager) Pete Waterman, and (Prince Rimshot) John 'Brad' Bradbury who along with the Lord Mayor and Pete Chambers unveiled it on 11th December. The plaque is on the side of the building facing the Precinct.

COV TRIVIA– The Gentleman's club to the left was once the infamous punk pub The Coventry Climax.

11. The Heath Hotel
807 Foleshill Road, CV6 5HS

> When you get here your iPod should be playing "Three Minute Hero"

Below The Heath as it was, and Neol (left) and Silverton do the honours. Photo by John Coles

Back in October 1977 the band that would become The Specials played their very first gig in this building. Jerry's own hand written diary of the time, states the band were called The Automatics (not The Hybrids as many think). He also mentions that the organ wouldn't fit on the stage, so he played it in the audience facing the band. This was in the pubs Rainbow Lounge supporting the punk bands Urban Blight, Certified, The Wild Boys (that included Roddy Byers and Squad (that included Terry Hall), but not for much longer.

"I think the 2-Tone Trail is important, because its Coventry's history, it's something for people of our age to enjoy and for the young people to learn about". **Silverton Hutchinson, Coventry Automatics**

Sponsored by Ska Band Special Brew
The Heath Hotel is not in walking distance of the Coventry city centre, so this one is just for the motorists and the die-hards. At the time of going to press the number 20 bus served the Foleshill Rd. The Heath (now the Wonder Years Day Nursery) is close to the Blue Ribbon Island on the A444. This plaque was unveiled by The Specials original drummer Silverton Hutchinson and Neol Davies (The Selecter) on 6th November 2009.

COV TRIVIA– Jerry Dammers and Tim Strickland were very close to coming to Coventry to unveil this plaque with Neol and Silverton, as Jerry liked the idea of having the original members together for this plaque. Sadly it didn't work out.

Non-plaque 2-Tone sites (marked as letters on map) Part 5

H-The Butts Stadium (Butts Road). This is a new stadium you see today, home of Coventry's Rugby team. In 1981, when racial tension in Britain was at a high, a Festival Against Racism was organised by Jerry Dammers on June 20th 1981, (Dammers had been primarily motivated after seeing an Asian doctor Amal Dharry stabbed to death at his local fish and chip shop in Broomfield Rd). It was to be an all day charity concert held at the Butts Stadium. The line up that day was The People, The Bureau, The Reluctant Stereotypes, Hazel O'Connor and The Specials. "The biggest thrill for me as a performer", said Hazel O'Connor. "Was playing alongside The Specials at The Butts when in spite of threats from the misanthropic right - a wonderful concert took place and people came out to show solidarity against the racist climate of that time". The New National Front picked that day to march in the City and some Earlsdon residents fought tooth and nail to get the concert cancelled, but despite the rain and the poor turn-out it proved a great day for local music and local common sense. It was the very last time all the original Specials would ever play together in their home city.

I-The Butts Technical College (Butts Road). A place of learning by day and entertainment at night. It was here that Horace, Jerry and Neol would watch artists like the Average White Band and ultimate reggae band Misty In Roots (who were originally Nicky Thomas's backing band). Neol also got to play here with his short-lived project named Castrovalva (named after a M. C. Escher lithograph). Today it's a hotel and the Wonderful Albany Theatre.

Specials play the Butts, photo Pete Chambers

Non-plaque 2-Tone sites (marked as letters on map) Part 6

J-The Domino Restaurant (Lower Precinct) This is where Jerry one night asked Roddy to join the Specials. Indeed, the next day a rather hung-over Roddy was awoken by Jerry Dammers and Pete Waterman hammering at his front door, eager to get to London to record a demo tape (the songs recorded were: Jaywalker, Too Much Too Young, Little Bitch and Dawning Of A New Era.) Lynval reveals it was a favourite of his:"Late nights at The Domino doing what all the youth would do at that time of night, drinking beer, getting drunk and chasing girls". The Specials played here on 5th December 1978.

K– Queens Rd Car Park/Ramada Hotel (Queens Rd) Once a car park next to Telecom Tower, now part of the Ramada Hotel. It was here that Jeff Veitch would take some of the first ever Specials promo photos. They were used on the Coventry Automatics album "Dawning Of A New Era". When the English Beat came to play at 2-Tone Central in 2012 they stopped at this hotel.

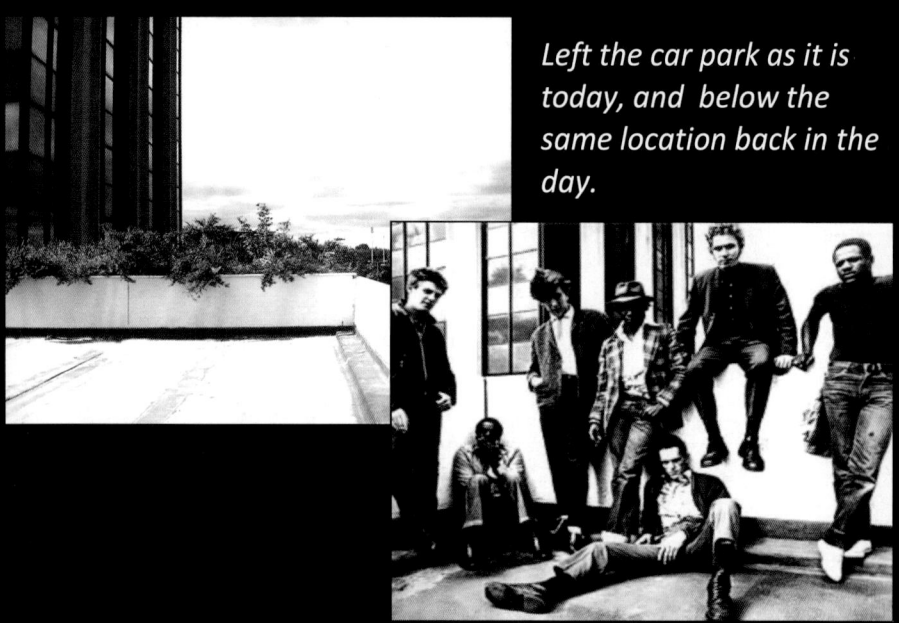

Left the car park as it is today, and below the same location back in the day.

Non-plaque 2-Tone sites (marked as letters on map) Part 7

L-The Dog and Trumpet (Hertford Street) A subterranean pub that began life as a Beer Keller and became a major venue in the town. The newly named Specials played here on Thursday 30th November 1978. Bad Manners played here a few times, as did General Public who included former 2-Tone troopers, Horace Panter from the Specials, Dave Wakeling and Ranking Roger from the Beat as well as Micky Billingham from Dexy's Midnight Runners. The Swinging Cats reformed and played a gig here in 2009. Of late, this venue seems to open under new names and ownership, then close again.

Above, One of the earliest and rarest photos of The Specials. Taken by Gary McGowan, at The Dog & Trumpet in 1978

M-The General Wolfe (Foleshill Road) The Specials rehearsed the routine for the Ghost Town video here, and The Selecter also rehearsed here. it was normal to spot a least one Special here on a gig night. The Wolfe was a major Coventry venue for local talent, probably the most important rock venue in the City. Indeed when Visit Britain published their England Rocks map in 2007, Coventry only got two mentions, one for 2-Tone, and the other for the General Wolfe! Former Manager Ken Brown had a long stint at the 'Wolfe' and booked a plethora of bands on its small but perfectly formed stage (even U2 played there in September 1980). The late 50's rocker Bob Davidson tried to revive it in 2009, but it never gained its musical credentials, it is currently a steak house.

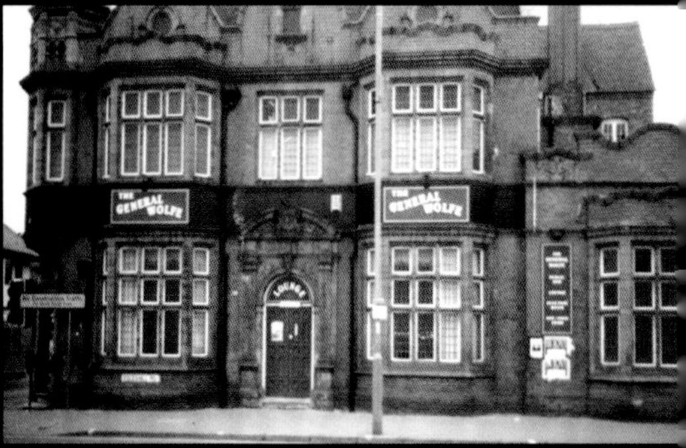

N-Grantham St, Brad lived in this street for many years opposite Gosford Green park in the Stoke district of Coventry.

O-Nerve Boutique (69, Queen Victoria Road) Trendy clothes shop Nerve. "The shop was started by Clare (my Wife) in 1981". Reveals Horace, "and I joined her as part of my 'Rock'N'Roll decompression strategy after being totally fed up with music after I left the Specials in the spring of 1982

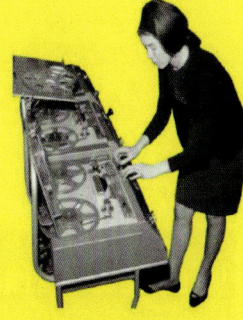

Welcome to The Delian Way, a do-it-yourself tour around the key places in Delia Derbyshire's Coventry.

She will always be remembered as the Electronic Music pioneer that gave us the iconic Doctor Who theme. Her genius was more than just one piece of music of course, although in that one piece of music a million thoughts have been thought and a million dreams been dreamt, not to mention the nostalgia trip it has brought us in the more recent times. So enjoy the trail, soak up the atmosphere, and please respect all the places on here.

Head to www.covmm.co.uk/DelianTrail for the companion Information site and map.

Lottery funded as part of #BigCelebration
www.biglotteryfund.org/celebrate

This was a community project led by Pete Chambers BEM, with Andy Holdcroft, Carole Quinney, Tony Seaton, The Coventry Society, Councillor Linda Bigham, Councillor Gary Ridley Andi Wolf and Paul Maddocks.

Special thanks to Carole & Adrian Quinney and Dean Eastment

Delia's Birth Certificate

FE 386031

CERTIFIED COPY of an ENTRY
Pursuant to the Births and Deaths Registration Act 1953

THE COVENTRY MUSIC MUSEUM
74-80 Walsgrave Rd Coventry, CV2 4ED

Start your tour in the CMM. Here you will find a permanent exhibition display dedicated to the lady herself. It depicts a mock-up of the BBC Radiophonic Workshop with control desk. It was officially opened by her partner Clive Blackburn in 2015.

Included is her personal tape recorder and her own copy of The Dr Who Theme. The Delia@80 events were staged here for her 80th Birthday.

COVENTRY MUSIC WALL OF FAME
74-80 Walsgrave Rd Coventry, CV2 4ED

Look on the walls of the 2-Tone Village, and you will find a plaque dedicated to Delia.

In 2014 she was posthumously inducted into the Coventry Music Wall Of Fame, along with Delia fan and 2-Tone creator Jerry Dammers, with Delia's partner Clive Blackburn representing her.

Delia's Co[v

We do hope you enjoy walking in Delia's footsteps around her native Coventry. As you can see the locations are spread out across the city, so walking the tour is not recommended. Your own transport or buses and taxis are the perfect ways to get around. The Coventry Music Museum makes an ideal starting point, where Delia fans can help you with the Trail.

Please be considerate to the private properties on the trail.

Copyright Google Maps

ventry

Delia's partner Clive Blackburn opens the Delia Display at The CMM, not with scissors and ribbon, but with recording tape and a razor blade.

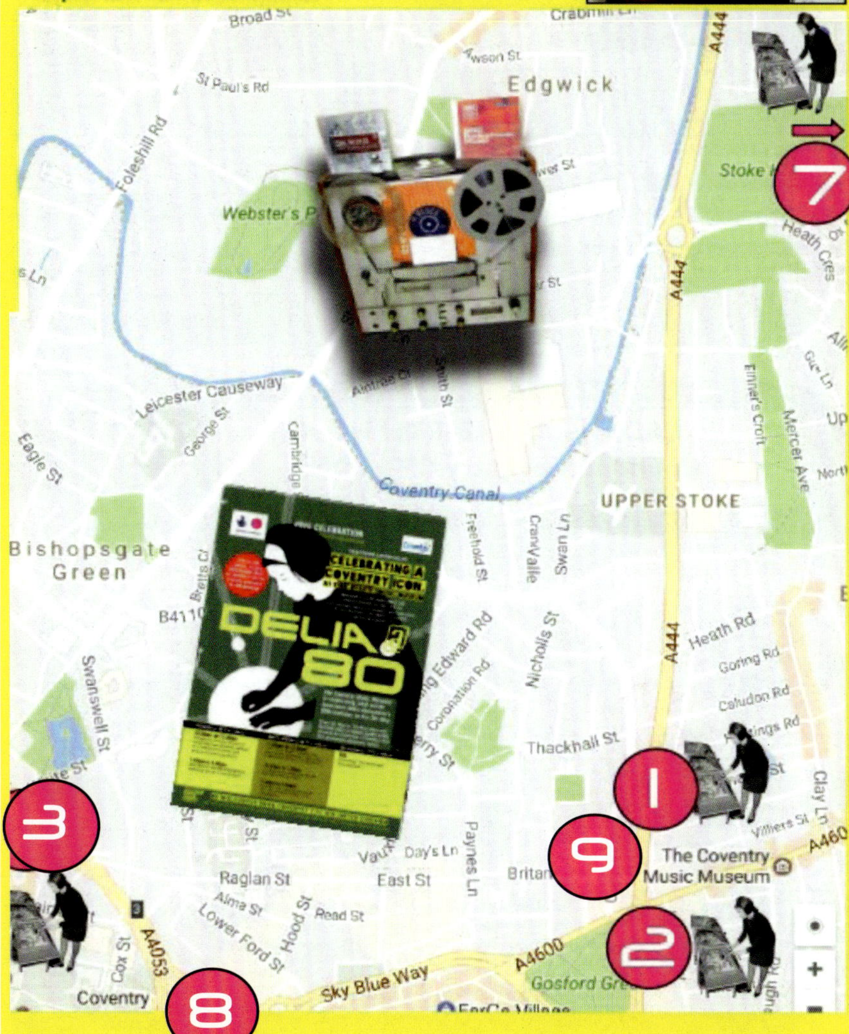

CATHEDRAL RUINS
Priory Street, Coventry, CV1 5FB

Once this was the majestic St Michael's Cathedral, but sadly destroyed in the blitz, an event that helped to create abstract sounds that would influence Delia later in life.

Objects like the air raid siren and the all clear, became her catalyst to Electronic music.

"*Coventry born, bred and blitzed.*" D. Derbyshire

124 CEDARS AVE (BIRTH HOME)
Coundon, Coventry, CV6 1DN

Delia was born here 5th May 1937. At the age of three she moved a little further up the road to 104.

A plaque organised by The Coventry Society was unveiled here on 5th May 2018 by her White Noise collaborator David Vorhaus

104 CEDARS AVE (CHILDHOOD HOME)
Coundon, Coventry, CV6 1DN

Delia grew up in 104, living here until she was 19 when she went to Cambridge. It was in the loft of this house many of Delia's belongings were found.

On 15th June 2017, as voted by the public, a BBC plaque was erected here. Unveiled by Clive Blackburn and Dr Who Colin Baker.

BARRS HILL SCHOOL
Radford Road, Coventry, CV1 4BU

Delia attended Barrs Hill in the late forties and early fifties. She unsurprisingly excelled at mathematics, she didn't study music in any depth at school, she described it as her "favourite hobby" though.

Her piano playing however was considered to be up to performance level.

DERBYSHIRE WAY
Stoke Heath, Coventry, CV2 3FA

The Museum is proud to have taken part in a campaign that saw a street be named after Delia. "Derbyshire Way" as part of the Delia @ 80 celebrations. This new road, is part of the "Brambles" estate, Stoke Heath. Although we never got her full name, we did manage to get "Way" included instead the proposed "Road", to give it a dual meaning, of that "Delian Way".

DELIA WALL ART
BY STEWY

8- In March 2018, renown urban artist Stewy began his Delia project. This included a initial black on white painting at The Ellen Terry Building exit door.
34-35 Jordan Well, CV1 5RW

9- The same day he painted a second Delia image, this time black on yellow and white at the entrance to The 2-Tone Village 74-80 Walsgrave Rd CV2 4ED

Other sites of interest

Christ The King, Catholic Church, Westhill Rd, Coventry, CV6 2AA
On opening the box of delights found at 104 Cedars Ave, it contained many items that referenced Christ The King.

Christ The King, Junior School, Scot's Lane, Coventry, CV6 2DJ
This was Delia's primary school.

Coventry Cathedral, Priory Street, Coventry, CV1 5FB
Venue for DeliaPhonic a concert to celebrate her 80th Birthday. In November 2017, Delia was awarded an Honorary Doctorate by Coventry University, the ceremony took place at the Cathedral.

The Tin, Canal Basin, Coventry CV1 4LY
Venue that regularly puts on Delia related events.

Site of Leofric Hotel, Broadgate, CV1 1LZ
Probably the last time Delia came to her birth-city. She was a guest at the Doctor Who convention Panopticon '98' in October 1998. Guests said she was happy to sign autographs and be recognised for her achievements. The building still stands, and has just recently been turned into student accommodation.

Right, seen here for the first time a very rare Delia's Birthday postcard from 1948. hand written by Delia herself. Showing Delia (with medal) at Christ The King, Junior School at her eleventh Birthday party. Bottom right all the gang, including Betty West who kindly donated this picture to us.

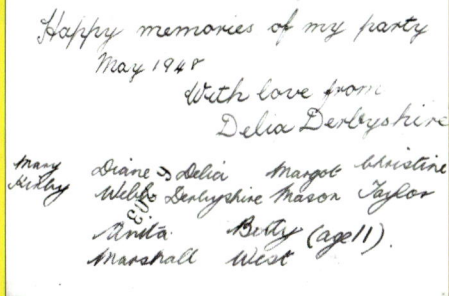

Left, another totally unseen photo of Delia (right) and her Sister Benita as they are confirmed at Christ The King. Benita passed away at the age of five. Photos from Barbara Yannall

The Enemy's Coventry

The Enemy, Coventry indie trio, remain the only Coventry artist to achieve a number one album. No longer a band, but their history lives on

#1 The Colosseum
Primrose Hill St
Something of a spiritual home, the band played here on many occasions including an appearance with ex-Specials vocalist Neville Staple. It was in the 'Colly' dressing room toilet where they read the graffiti, "We'll Live and Die In these Towns"

#2 The Herbert
Jordan Well
One of the first venues to give The Enemy a gig, The Enemy featured here on the displays and in interviews when the museum hosted the "More Than Two Tones" exhibition in 2009.

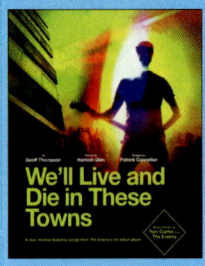

#3 Sports Centre
Fairfax Street
Much of the "It's Not OK" video was shot with the band playing on the roof of the Sports Centre, next to the swimming baths,. The soon to be demolition building is shaped like an elephant, the civil symbol of the city.

#4 The Empire
Gosford Street
This nightclub/venue is co-Managed by Tom Clarke. The Empire has hosted The Enemy on several occasions including their very last three superb gigs in 2016.

Above, the poster for the Enemy play written by Geoff Thompson, with Tom Clarke as musical Director that debuted at The Belgrade Theatre 2018.

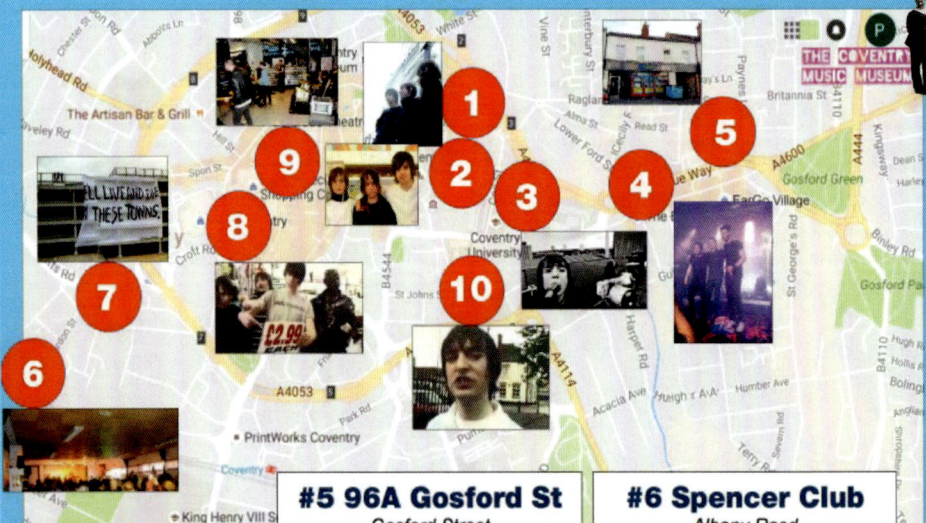

#5 96A Gosford St
Gosford Street
Tom's flat above William Hill betting shop, where Tom wrote, "We'll Live and Die In These Towns". Whilst introducing "Live and Die" on stage during the final gigs at The Empire, Tom gave his old flat a shout out.

#6 Spencer Club
Albany Road
The Spencer Club was one of the popular city venues where The Bridges played, others included The Jailhouse and The Cottage in Earlsdon.

#7 Ramada Car Park
Butts

The car park featured in the video It's Not OK, where the huge, "We'll Live and Die" banner is unfurled. The car park was also the chosen location of the early Coventry Automatics photographs, when it was part of the Post Office building.

#8 Coventry Market
Queen Victoria Road

A large part of the video "40 Days and 40 Nights" was filmed in the iconic 'round' of Coventry's retail market, where Tom, Andy and Liam, scare pigeons, juggle fruit and finally reveal they are worth £2.99 each.

#11 Godiva Festival
War Memorial Park

This was the festival that pretty much defined the band. In 2006 they began as unknowns, 2007 went on to smash it in the rhythm tent, finally headlining in 2008.

#12 Venus Fish Bar
Queen Victoria Road

The Specials had The Parsons Nose, The Enemy had their local chippy The Venus, as featured in the video for "40 Days and 40 Nights". Incidentally The Parsons Nose makes an appearance in "It's Not OK".

Tom Clarke now as a solo artist and Andy Hopkins and his band Autopilot, made a return to The Godiva Festival, ten years on from their first gig there.

From 2007, The Enemy were ubiquitous around Coventry. Like The 2-Tone bands before, this hit making band had inspired their hometown, and we were as proud of them, as they of us. Enemy at HMV, at the train station and CMM.

#9 HMV
Precinct & Hertford St

The Enemy have made several guest appearances (playing live and album signing) at HMV Coventry. Including its Hertford Street and Precinct locations. The present HMV in the Precinct is in a new location, and has never hosted the band.

#10 Hope & Anchor
Whitefriars Lane

A long gone venue. Some of their first gigs happened here. Warner Brothers Records came here to see the band and the BBC came here to do a piece about the band. The live scenes of the video "40 days and 40 Nights" were also filmed here.

#13 Radio 1 Live Lounge

It was broadcasted from Liam's parents home in Holbrooks on 13th December 2007. With DJ Jo Whiley in attendance, the band played a cover of Cyndi Lauper's "Girls just Want To Have Fun" with Last Christmas and Leona Lewis's "Bleeding Love" thrown in for good measure.

#14 The Ricoh
Phoenix Way

It was here, under the CCFC club crest, where the band signed their recording contract with John Dawkins. The band played a memorable concert here in 2008, with the then Lord Mayor in attendance.

The band also famously supported Oasis here too.

"Holbronx"

HOLBROOKS

In 2012, the Olympics came to Coventry, and we got to host some of the football matches at the Ricoh Arena, rebranded as the Coventry Stadium for the Olympics. As part of the cultural events we were asked by Coventry City Council to broaden The 2-Tone Trail to include other non 2-Tone music sites in the city. So we created The Coventry Rocks Music Tour and it ran from June to September in 2012 and was sponsored by Coventry City Council and Coventry Market.

The tour met at the **Cathedral and Cathedral Ruins**
Despite anyone's spiritul leanings the Cathedral is pretty much the heart of Coventry for most Coventrians. Although music has always been part of this magnifiecent building too. Not just organ music and hymns, popular music has always been not only accepted here, but encouraged too (it still is, with recent Ska and Rock concerts taking place here). In the year 1962 Benjamin Britten's War Requiem had its debut here for the consecration ceremony for the new cathedral. In 1966 Jazz legend Duke Ellington performed in the new cathedral, in 1971 German Electronic band Tangerine Dream not only performed here, but released a film of the concert. Classic guitarist John Williams also played here.

In the Cathedral ruins King played for Saturday Super Store see photo above, The Enemy tried but never did, in the 70's Ra-HoTep played a fundraiser in the ruins for the Coventry Diggers, a group of local hippies. Many others have also played here even Tinchy Stryder.

Duke Ellington

Map by Robert Orland

Cathedral and Cathedral Ruins Continued

John Lennon and Yoko Ono came to Coventry to plant two acorns at the Cathedral on 15th June 1968. There is a lot more information on this in the "Beatles Sent From Coventry" section of this very book. Yoko came back in 2005, and planted two oak trees that are growing well in the Cathedral grounds.

Walk of Stars (Priory Place, outside the BBC)

It was an idea of mine to see something tangible in Coventry that was dedicated to The Specials. The selection was done on a voting system, but I knew The Specials were bound to be one of the chosen inductees. I was right, and the Specials were inducted along with many other famous very Coventrians (or those with a massive link to the city), on May 16th (the Day Coventry won the 1987 FA Cup) in 2008 and 2009. This is a rebranding to the original project, other names include The Selecter, Pete Waterman OBE, Vince Hill, Hazel O'Connor, Lady Godiva, Sir Frank Whittle, Coventry City 1987 FA Cup Winners, Marlon Devonish, Sir Nigel Hawthorne, Sir Alfred Herbert, Mo Mowlam, Jimmy Hill OBE, Dave Moorcroft OBE, James Starley, Sir Henry Parkes, Sir William Lyons, Philip Larkin, Clive Owen and Billie Whitelaw.

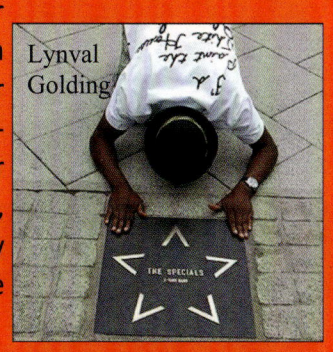

The Alahambra Public House (New Buildings)

On the tour, we walked past the site of this long gone pub on the tour, so it was it a good chance to mention licensee Don Fardon who not only owned this pub, but was part of the Coventry Beat band The Sorrows who had a top thirty hit with "Take A Heart" in 1965. He also had a pretty good solo career with the hits, "Indian Reservation" and the ode to George Best "Belfast Boy". The Sorrows reformed a few years back to spread their Mod Freakbeat sound around and they have just announced their retirement.

Black Eagle Pub Now A Chinese Restaurant, this jazz and blues venue was once part of the Leofric Hotel. Famous for its "Sunday Session R&B Club" of the 1960's. Legends like Chris Farlowe, Cliff Bennett, Zoot Money, Long John Baldry, Jeff Beck, Spooky Tooth and Reggae legend Jimmy Cliffe all played here. There was also a legendary night in 1968, when host Jimmy Tarbuck   apprenty got up to jam with Pete Green's Fletwood Mac.

Locarno/Tiffany's It's Central Library now, but was once a thriving venue and dance hall lovingly christened "The Rockhouse" where many Coventrians met their partners. From early Irish Showband dances, to the beat generation (hosting bands like The Rolling Stones and The Who). Its famous revolving stage was walked upon by many famous feet. In 1971 Led Zepplin played during the famous bomb scare, where many left and many didn't , Robert and the boys just kept on playing, it turned out to be a hoax. Pete Waterman was making a name for himself as DJ extrodinaire. In 1972, Chuck Berry came along as part of the Lanchester Arts Festival and recorded his only number one, the less than classic "My Ding-A-Ling" his only chart topper. In the audience that night were Jerry Dammers, Lene Lovich and from the support band Slade, Noddy Holder. Noddy likes to say,: "People say I sang on six number ones, wrong I sang on seven, I was in the audience and sang on My Ding-A-Ling too".

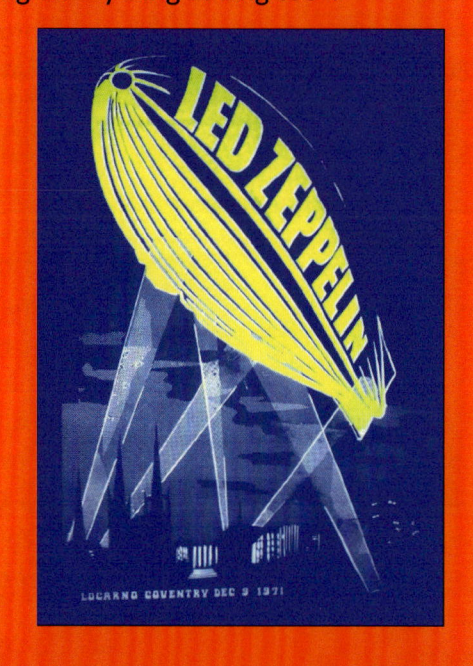

Chuck Berry at The Locarno

Locarno/Tiffany's Continued The Clash, Human League, The Jam, Blondie and The Stranglers all played here. In the late 70's and early 80's all the 2-Tone bands of the time played there, including two very Special Specials homecomings in 1979. Live B-sides "Skinhead Symphony" The Specials and "Carry Go Bring Home" by The Selecter, were both recorded here. The Locarno is also immortalised in the lyrics of The Specials song "Friday Night, Saturday Morning". It eventually closed as a venue and became Coventry's Central library, that means it is still very open to the public and they even have the odd gig here between the shelves of books.

Charlie of the Selecter at the rear of Tiffany's with fans, photo courtesy of Toni Tye

Lower Precinct Two main sites here, The Domino a bar and restaurant that stayed open later than most of the other pubs, it was the place to be for Cov's muso's, including would-be-Specials (see the 2-Tone Trail for more) it's now a soap shop. Then we have Mr George nightclub that gave The Coventry Automatics a recidency (see the 2-Tone Trail for more), it's now a TJ Hughes, the New Look shop next door was Cov's C&A, but I don't have a say.

The Domino

Busters Long gone night club that was effectively a bridge across the lower part of Market Way. Lots of bands played here, I recall Pete Shelley fresh out of the Buzzcocks bring the house down.

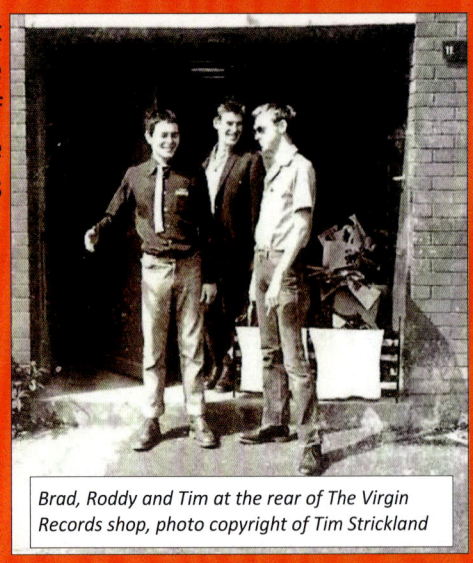

Brad, Roddy and Tim at the rear of The Virgin Records shop, photo copyright of Tim Strickland

City Arcade Site of the original Virgin Records shop, here worked original Automatics vocalist Tim Strickland, and the late great John 'Brad' Bradbury. The room above was The Soul Hole run by Pete Waterman, if you wanted a hard to-find-record, he could get it for you. One of Coventry's most celebrated photographers John Coles also worked here. See the 2-Tone Trail for more information.

Holyhead Youth Club This was the place where Sound System DJ's Neville Staple and Trevor Evans and The Specials first 'heard' each other. Eventually resulting in Neville and Trevor Evans becoming the Specials road crew, and for Neville to be part of the band. See The 2-Tone Trail for more information.

The Belgrade Theatre One of the finest provincial theatres in the land. As part of the Lanchester Festival 1971, The Monty Python team performed live for the very first time right here. Local artists like Hazel O'Connor and Vince Hill have appeared here. Bob Eaton's "Three Minute Hero" play has been on here twice, local music based play "Godiva Rocks" made its debut here. The Enemy play "We'll Live & Die" written by Geoff Thompson debuted here.

Three Minute Hero play photo by John Coles

Coventry Theatre

Major Coventry venue long gone, but the Beatles played here (see Beatles Sent To Coventry), The Stones, Laurel & Hardy, Elton John, Bowie, Queen, King, Vince Hill, Frank Ifield, Pink Floyd, Roy Orbison and Jimi Hendrix, and any other of the 'greats' you can think of. The area where it stood is now the frontage to the wonderful Coventry Transport Museum. Actually, part of The Coventry Theatre was a small shop that eventually became **Poster Place**. Everyone of a certain age bought their posters, gig tickets, gig photos, patches and badges from here, it even introduced a 2-Tone badge swop scheme. We hear it mentioned in the music museum so many times, always with nostalgic sadness of its decline. Last act on its stage before it became a bingo hall was Barbra Dixon 6th June 85. it was demolished in 2002. There is a plaque on the site to commerate its existence.

The Orchid, Tic Toc, Colly now the Kasbah

Coventry's only real constant of a venue, from the 60's, 80's and onwards, The 60's was alive with beat music, so local entrepreneur Larry Page took over the Orchid Ballroom in Primrose Hill Street and strived to create a Coventry Sound to rival Mersey Beat and Brum Beat. Larry Page's roster of artists including three teenage Stoke Park School Girls "The Orchids" christianed after the venue and signed to Decca Records. The Pickwicks, Shel Naylor, were also on Decca and managed by Larry Page.

In the 80's shock shock to be, Jon Gaunt ran it as the Tic Toc, The Selecter played here are recorded a live album here (see the 2-Tone Trail).

As The Colosseum In 2007, it became something of a spiritual home to the Enemy (see The Enemy's Coventry).

As the Kasbah it continues to host great music and great acts including PIL, N-Dubz, Babyshambles, Artic Monkeys, la Roux and Calvin Harris.

The Golden Cross The oldest pub in Coventry and always ready to rock . In 2005, The Golden Cross was used as the venue for the debut gig of a new band formed on the TV series Rock School. The host was Kiss's multi-millionaire rock god Gene Simmons, who apparently saw the Coventry Cathedral spire, and inquired if it was for sale, he was also wondering why the Cathedral ruins windows had not been repaired.

THE COVENTRY ROCKS MUSIC TOUR.........

THE BEATLES
SENT TO COVENTRY
TOUR

The Beatles' Coventry

Looking for somewhere to soak up some Beatle-vibe in Coventry and area has become a harder job since the 'ultimate' Beatle place in Coventry, namely The Coventry Theatre was torn down. The site of the theatre is at the northern foot of the spectacular Whittle Arch, in front of the equally spectacular Coventry Transport Museum.

1. Brooklands Farm Hotel
Now The Jacobean Hotel, Holyhead Road, Coventry.
It is accepted by many local Beatles fans to be the Hotel the Moptops rested their er..moptops after their November 1963 gig at Coventry Theatre. The hotel's advertising once said, that if you listen very hard during a visit, you can hear the voice of John Lennon in the corridors. The present owners are to change all that as they are unsure that the boys ever stayed here.

Though there is no smoke without fire. In November 1963 the word got about to fans that this is where they would stay. The then manager Fredrick Tyler told the Coventry Express, "We must have has 150 phone calls asking for tickets, why would they pick on us I don't know".

"The Beatles are not staying here, In fact I don't think they are staying in Coventry on Sunday night". One gang of teenagers threatened to camp out on the hotel's grounds until they were given tickets! The Manager seemed to be well informed of the Beatles movements though, and if they were stopping there, he was hardly going to advertise the fact was he?

Robert & Lesley Jackson former owners of the Brooklands farm Hotel

The Route into Coventry, *Coventry Theatre show November 17TH 1963*

The Police officer in charge of "Operation Beatle" Superintendent E. Townsend he was taking no chances as far as Beatle security went. "Everyone was expecting gimmicks", he told the Coventry Evening Telegraph at the time, "So we went the other way and brought them in by the most direct route". The Beatles had left their Hotel at The Branksome Towers near Bournemouth late morning, stopping en route for a spot of lunch, before phoning ahead to Coventry Police station for further instructions. One of the police requirements was that they arrived at 3.30pm, before school ended. According to the Coventry Telegraph they missed the deadline by 30 minutes and got into Coventry at 4.00pm.

On arrival in Coventry they travelled in their Austin Princess car from Little Park Steet Police Station, down Hight St into Broadgate onto the Burges and then Hales Street straight into the back of the Coventry Theatre. Almost immediately barriers went up behind the car to protect the group from the 200 or so girls who had braved the winter rain to see their idols! Beatles road manager Neil Aspinall, was happy with Superintendent Townsend's handling of it all.

2. Coventry Cathedral
Coventry City Centre

Well so it was on 15th June 1968, John with Yoko Ono (mid way through recording *The White Album*, between the tracks *Blackbird* & *Revolution 9* to be exact) attended 'The National Sculpture Exhibition' in the grounds of Coventry Cathedral.

This was to be the couple's first 'real' time out in public together and first joint artistic venture, entitled '*Acorns For Peace,* or *Living Art-Two Acorns*, (they would later name-check acorns in the Beatles song *Ballad of John and Yoko,* when Lennon sings, "Fifty acorns tied in a sack"). As Coventry Cathedral was (and still is) a dominion of reconciliation and world peace, it was an obvious place for the couple to "perform" their peace-art. They turned up in John's long white Rolls Royce (with very advanced features for 1968 including TV, video recorder, 'floating' record player and Telephone). On the back was attached a trailer (a perfect example of Lennon's paradoxical life-style). On the trailer was a round white circular metal seat of two halves that when pushed together formed a circle. The intention was to sit on and contemplate the growing of the acorns beneath you. Natural art if you like. What could be more perfect than that? They would plant two acorns (in white plastic cups) in the centre of it, with one facing East, and one West, symbolising the meeting of John & Yoko, and their two different cultures. The day however was filled with problems.

First the couple's sculpture was banned from being shown in the main exhibit area in the ruins of the old Cathedral. Fabio Barraclough, who was the assistant of art at Rugby School and the chief organiser of the event, claimed that it was Canon Stephen Verney who had the sculpture moved because he objected to exhibiting their work on consecrated ground because of their extra-marital relationship. Canon Stephen Verney later refuted this claim. He was unhappy however about this metal bench and acorns being considered 'art' and the fact the couple had signed up for the exhibition at the last minute.

Photo Keith McMillian

Coventry Cathedral Acorn Event Probably because of that John and Yoko's exhibit was not mentioned in the main catalogue, so they produced their own, (basically one sheet folded making 4 pages, with a thin tissue paper cover) but even this was not allowed to be distributed. (I once owned a copy lent it to The Cathedral and never saw it again sadly) . In the privacy of the Deanery, Yoko became hysterical and was shouting at the Canon to ring leading artists (including Henry Moore who was not at home) to prove that their work was indeed 'art'!

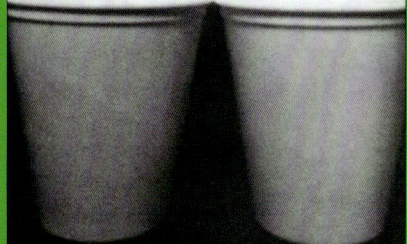

Top left cover of the programme, top right John & Yoko planting the acorns, Bottom left The couple trying out one of the other exhibits and above the author and Yoko in 2005.
Photos by Keith McMillian & Julie Chambers

The Ceremony

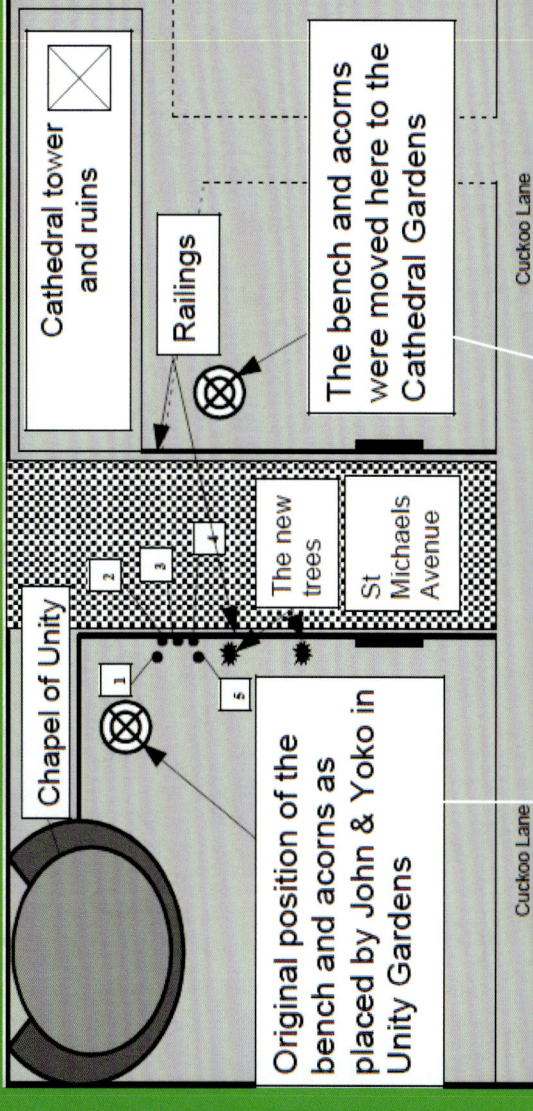

Positions of the major players during the "Acorn Discussions, 1968".

1. Fabio Barraclough
2. Yoko
3. John
4. Anthony Fawcett
5. Canon Verney

Cathedral tower and ruins

Railings

The bench and acorns were moved here to the Cathedral Gardens

Cuckoo Lane

Chapel of Unity

The new trees

St Michaels Avenue

Original position of the bench and acorns as placed by John & Yoko in Unity Gardens

Cuckoo Lane

Coventry Cathedral Acorn Event Continued The myths of that Saturday in June continue. Some say the couple were so upset they later sent some more acorns and they were put under 24 hour security (or armed guard as one US site claims). The bench/sculpture itself was later removed by Lennon's chauffeur Les Anthony and taken back down to Kenwood on the trailer.

John and Yoko are seen sitting on it briefly in the film Imagine (actually an extract from Yoko's film "Rape"). In 1984 when Strawberry Fields was opened in Central Park New York. Yoko mentioned that sixteen years earlier she and John had planted acorns in the precincts of Coventry Cathedral. That acorn was now symbolically a tree. So no matter what happened to those two little acorns, the Cathedral at Coventry is an important part of the John and Yoko story.

Yoko's Return October 14th 2005 So it was on Friday that Yoko Ono came back to our city and continued the work she and John Lennon had begun some 37 years and 4 months previously. As part of Coventry Peace Month, she dedicated two Japanese oak trees in the Cathedral gardens. As preparations for her arrival took place, I got to thinking that the scene that had occurred over 37 years previously had now been allowed out of its 'freeze frame state' and the film had finally been left to run.

When Yoko arrived though, all those lost years seemed to disappear. This time it went like clockwork. At around 3.30 Yoko arrived, without any bodyguards, just a team of very helpful aids, including Murray Chalmers, her very charming and professional press officer. The ceremony, itself held on Unity Lawn included a welcome from the then Lord Mayor Cllr Ram Lakah and the present Dean Of Coventry, The Very Rev John Irvine. Yoko symbolically un-knotted a silken rope wrapped around both of the already planted oak tree saplings.

Yoko Unties the rope, watched by Cllr Lakah.
Photo by Hannah Tobin

Coventry Theatre *Hales Street* A major Coventry venue where The Beatles played twice (24-2-63 & 17-11-63), head for the Coventry Transport Museum, before you get to the entrance head right. Turn the corner under the blue walk-way steps and you will come to Chauntry Place. Go inside and this side of the brick wall (before you get to the houses on the other side) is where the stage door of the theatre was located. Feel the vibes of those Mop Top Days, yeah, yeah, yeah.

Matrix *Fletchamstead Highway* Now a HSS Hire shop (not a car showroom as Mick Jagger announced on stage at the Ricoh). It's run by a good team of friendly guys who knew of the building's history, and were kind enough to show us the original flooring and the area where the stage was originally located. The Beatles played here 17th November 1962 (yeah the Fab Four played twice in Coventry on 17th November, the Museum celebrates Cov Beatles Day on 17th Nov). Post code is CV4 9BY

Fletch *Fletchamstead Highway* This was the pub where music legends to be Pete Waterman and The Beatles shared a drink, probably to cool the nerves, judging by Paul's comments on this gig from the Let It Be film. Being just a few yards from the Matrix, this was a regular watering whole for Matrix musicians and punters alike. This is now a car showroom so the inside has changed but outside, much of the former pub's character is intact. in July 1968 it was on this very road, where Paul picked up a speeding ticket. I doubt if Paul even made the Connection? The postcode is CV4 9BY by the way.

Right, it was only a few yards from the Matrix to The Fletch (and back again), please excuse the very contemporary clip art of the fab four.

The Matrix building

The Fletch Pub

Coventry's music mile

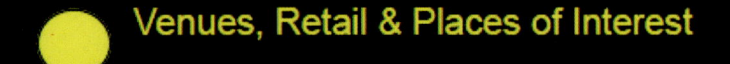

● **Venues, Retail & Places of Interest**

● **Music Shops**

○ **Historic Music Sites**

Swan Lane, Terry Hall lived Here. Mercers Arms, Gigs were hosted at CCFC

Grantham St John Bradbury lived

White Lion

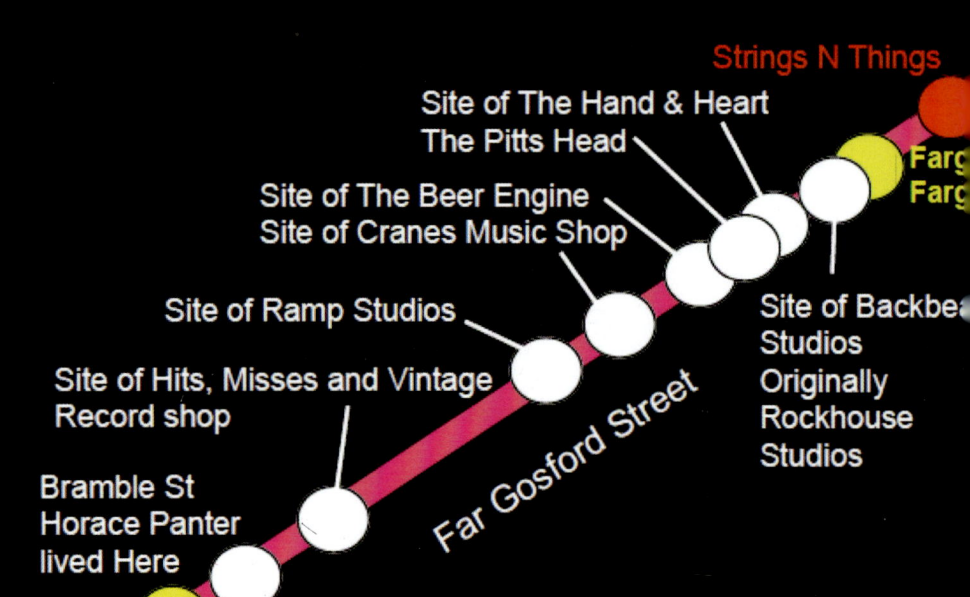

Strings N Things

Site of The Hand & Heart
The Pitts Head

Site of The Beer Engine
Site of Cranes Music Shop

Farg
Farg

Site of Ramp Studios

Site of Hits, Misses and Vintage Record shop

Site of Backbe. Studios
Originally Rockhouse Studios

Bramble St
Horace Panter lived Here

Far Gosford Street

Scholars

The Empire

THE EMPIRE COVENTRY

More of an idea than a real concept but a with a few banners and a information sheet and it could become the music quarter and a reality and another place of interest in the City of Culture.

COVENTRY MUSIC WALL OF FAME

The Coventry Music Wall of Fame, is located at the 2-Tone Village, well actually on the walls all around the Village to be exact. Each recipient (or their representative) has been part of one of the many ceremonies, and has been inducted onto the Wall of Fame. The first ceremony was on November 2011, when six local heroes were inducted, witnessed by the cameras of BBC Midlands Today no less. Many have followed them each on the wall for making an outstanding contribution to Coventry and Warwickshire music. The organising team included myself (Pete Chambers), Brody Swain, Pete Clemons, Councillor Tony Skipper and Mark Dixon. I was humbled to be awarded a surprise plaque in 2012, but had no knowledge of it, having received the third most votes on the peoples poll.

The names on the wall are: *Bob Brolly, Steve Eaton, Lynval Golding, Neol Davies, Panjabi MC, Vince Holliday, Pauline Black, Lieutenant Pigeon, Hazel O'Connor, Pete Chambers, Delia Derbyshire, Jerry Dammers, Ray King, Roddy Byers, Charley Anderson, Steve & Heather Taylor, Roger Lomas, John Bradbury, Vince Hill, The Primitives, Horace Panter, Paul Sampson, Steve Edgson, Trevor Evans, Taz Singh, Neville Staple, Frank Ifield, John Shipley, Gapps, Dave Willetts, Bobbie Clarke, The Sorrows, Bev Jones, Aitch Benbridge, Dave Swarbrick and The Enemy.* You can still make a vote by emailing it here (subject WOF) tencton@hotmail.com

Left the 1st WOF, *Bob Brolly, Steve Eaton, Lynval Golding, Neol Davies, Panjabi MC, Vince Holliday, Right 5th WOF With Clive Blackburn (for Delia), Jerry Dammers & Ray King*

Discovering the areas of Coventry– so you can be like a local

Binley, The late Specials drummer John Bradbury attended Binley Park School as did Specials fan and superstar actor Clive Owen and Mark Rattray, the last person to win Opportunity Knocks. Baroque composer Capel Bond is buried at St Bartholomews church. King vocalist Paul King was a minstrel at Coombe Abbey medieval banquet. Rumour has it that David Bowie once stopped at the Coombe Abbey Hotel.

Canley, The Matrix Ballroom was here, The Beatles played this venue (see The Beatles Sent To Coventry) (now a tool hire shop), strangely years later Macca got a speeding ticket on the Fletchamstead Highway. The Fletch pub (now a car showroom) once served The Beatles pre-Matrix gig beers. Jasper Carrott recoded half of his "Rabbitts On and On" LP at The Fletch pub. Canley College was an early venue for The Coventry Automatics. The University of Warwick is also here, and many fine bands have played at The Arts Centre and The Copper Rooms, Sting and Simon Mayo are alumni. The Jam's first non-London gig was at Canley Teachers Training College in 1976.

Cheylsmore, During the Fun Boy 3 days Lynval Golding lived at Esher Drive. Cheylesmore Youth Club is featured in the music video of the "4 my city" by former Coventry Hip Hop band "City Ov Villanz" .

City Centre, Cov Theatre, Belgrade, The Locarno, The Lanch, Mr George were all city centre clubs and venues, there were lots of others of course. Music Hall star T. E. Dunville was born in New Street and grew up in Lower Ford Street. King were like a fish out of water because the ring road lead them round and around, the ring road was again immortalised in song as part of a BBC CWR project as was Coventry Market (and later featured on Harry Hill's Show). Coventry Market was the scene for the Roddy song "Concrete Jungle" as used in the BBC2 documentary. It had a stall dedicated to 2-Tone in 2009, it now has the only vinyl shop in Cov. The Eclipse became home to the UK's first city centre legal all night raves. The Coventry Stars, are based outside BBC CWR. As I write HMV is once again in trouble.

Coundon, Birthplace of Delia Derbyshire (see The Delian Way) in Cedars Ave, Birthplace of Frank Ifield at 98 Evenlode Crescent. The Legendary broadcaster Brian Matthew attended Bablake School.

The 2-Tone Village (The Coventry Music Museum, Coventry Music Wall of Fame, Knights Venue, Hall of Fame Memorabillia, 2-Tone Cafe & 2-Tone Corner Shop)

THE COVENTRY MUSIC MUSEUM

The Old Ball Hotel

Site of St Margaret's Cafe

St Michael's Rd Paul King lived Here

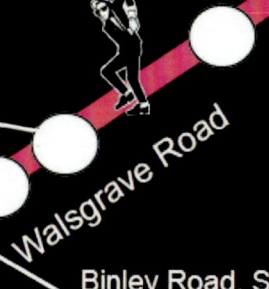

Kingsway Lieutenant Pigeon Recorded Here, including the song "Gosford Street Rag"

Walsgrave Road

Binley Road, Site of The Stoker, Bulls Head, Express Music

Noise Works

Tom Clarke wrote "We'll Live and Die" when he lived here

llage (Comfy Bookshop, cooters and The Box)

WE ARE Coventry 2021 UK CITY OF CULTURE

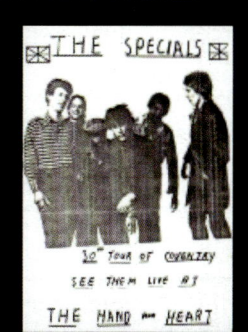

FARGO creative village

THE COVENTRY MUSIC MUSEUM

The 2-Tone Village
Coventry www.2tonecentral.co.uk
LIVE MUSIC VENUE-SHOPPING-COVENTRY MUSIC WALL OF FAME-FASHION
MEMORABILIA-COVENTRY MUSIC MUSEUM-CAFE-RESTAURANT-RECORDS

Pauline & Gapps at museums' "Wall of Hits", centre "Rude Boys Bedroom" and Stranger Cole (middle) gets his star from Christine & Neville Staple.

The museum has remained in the top two of Trip Advisor's "Things to do in Coventry" for over four years. It's open 10.00am to 4.00pm Thursdays to Saturdays last entry at 3.30pm and 10.00am to 3.00 on Sundays and Bank Holidays last entry at 2.30pm. Entrance fee is £3.00 for adults, £2 concessions and £1.00 for children (aged 5-15). It can be found in the Stoke, Ball Hill area of Coventry, Walsgrave Road, CV2 4HY, it is part of the famous 2-Tone Village. Expect some amazing new displays for 2019 (40 years of 2-Tone) and for 2021 (City of Culture) For more information go to www.covmm.co.uk or phone 07971171441

The **2-Tone Village** was created for the fans by the fans, and as well as the award winning music museum, it includes the 2-Tone Corner sub-culture shop, Hall of Fame memorabilia store. The 2-Tone café and the award winning Simmer Down Caribbean restaurant and Knights live venue and wine bar, plus the Coventry Music Wall of Fame and the Stars of Ska & Reggae wall . It's the musical heart of Coventry.

People behind the **Stars of Ska & Reggae Wall** are Suky Singh, Neville and Christine Staple and Rich Lock. It's one place in Britain where our Ska and Reggae roots are celebrated. Prince Buster, Alton Ellis, Susan Cadogan, Rico Rodriguez MBE and Stranger Cole have all been inducted on the wall, with more to come. In November 2018 the **Iconic Visitors Wall** was launched and Jam drummer Rick Buckler became the first person to be on there, as you can see, lots to do at the 2-Tone Village.

More Areas of Coventry 2

Earlsdon, Cov's Arty area, various Specials lived here (Jerry at 51 Albany Rd, 2-Tone HQ). Birthplace of Roddy Byers. Earlsdon Festival takes place here every summer. The Albany Social Club has hosted many a gig, Nexus Institute of Creative Arts is based in the area. During the Fun Boy 3 days Terry Hall lived at Michaelmas Rd and Neville Staple at Broomfield Rd.

Foleshill, Panjabi MC's family business is in Foleshill as are Planet Studios and World Music Recording Studios, Grammy award winning producer Roger Lomas grew up here. The late lamented General Wolfe venue was here too, currently this icon is a steakhouse. The would-be Specials played their first gig as The Coventry Automatics at The Heath (see The 2-Tone Trail).

Green Lane, Moat Avenue, HQ for late 70's, early 80's fanzine Alternative Sounds run by Martin Bowes. Under Kenpass Highway, the Green Lane underpass murals had some great art gracing its walls depicting The Specials, that was back in 2008, I'm guess by now it's been tagged on now many times or been removed.

Hillfields, Former Specials front man Neville Staple lived here. The Selecter based themselves here at Charley Anderson's flat in Pioneer House tower block in Adelaide St (the 16th tallest building in Coventry if you're interested) the building was featured in the play "Three Minute Hero". Terry Hall attended Sidney Stringer School. Hillfields is name checked in the song "Fearful" composed by Horace Panter from the 1998 album Guilty 'Til Proved Innocent! The Kasbah is still located here, The punk fave The Swanswell pub is no longer a pub, currently an ice cream parlour. The superb Hillz FM community radio is based in Hillfields Square.

Holbrooks, Broadcaster & singer Bob Brolly lived here, Vince Hill was born here and sang at The Hen Lane Club. The Enemy lived here (see The Enemy's Coventry). It's close to the Ricoh Arena, The Enemy and the Specials have both played there, as well as Oasis, Bruce Springsteen, Bon Jovi, Take That, The Rolling Stones (supported by the Specials) and the first singer to do so Bryan Adams. Pre 2-Tone band Nite Train that included Ray King, Neol Davies and Jerry Dammers once rehearsed at the The Bantam.

More areas of Coventry 3

Kersley, Roddy Byers lived here. Specials fan Clive Own was born here. In 2006 Norwegian trio A-Ha played a secret gig at the Old Shepherd pub.

Longford, Hazel O'Connor attended Foxford School, in 2016 she was honoured by her former school with a lifetime achievement award. The school later opened the award out to non-Foxford Alumni and awarded former Specials vocalist Neville Staple the award in 2017.

Radford, Beverley Jones got a lucky break at the Craftman pub in Radford in the late fifties. The Pilot was a pub that helped launch The Sorrows and the 2-Tone movement, in the 70's Neol Davies and John Bradbury held a jazz club here. Original Specials drummer Silverton lived in Burnaby Road and the band often rehearsed at his home. Squad name-checked the area in their song "Millionaire" when they were hanging around with the Radford boys. Delia Derbyshire attended Barrs Hill School, (see The Delian Trail), as did All About Eve vocalist Julianne Regan and Coventry rapper Whizzy.

Spon End, The Sky Dome ice rink is occasionally used for concerts including UB40. The long gone Glasshouse (Upper York Street) Studio opened in 1982, this education based audio recording facility was set up by Charlie Anderson, Lynval Golding and former Hardtop 22 man Amos Anderson. This is also the location of the Butts stadium where the Specials played their last gig in Coventry with their original line up, the city is calling out for them to return to the Butts to play a concert for the 40th anniversary.

Stivichall, The yearly Godiva Festival (featured the likes of The Enemy, Hazel O'Connor, Neville Staple Band, The Stranglers, The Buzzcocks, Human League and The Boomtown Rats and many more) takes place every summer at the War Memorial Park. The BBC Biggest Weekend 2018 gave us Liam Gallagher, The Stereophonics and Paloma Faith. The annual Caribbean Festivals was also held here at the Memorial Park. Jerry Dammers, Creator of The 2-Tone movement went to school at Henry VIII, as did John Shipley of Special AKA Fame and also the man that created Grindcore and Napalm Death Nick Bullen.